MW00791107

# WHEN THE MAN YOU LOVE TREATS YOU LIKE THE WOMAN HE HATES

*How to deal with abusive behavior*
*from those you love the most*

Dr. David B. Hawkins, ACSW, Ph.D.

"*Perfect love drives out fear.*"

—1 JOHN 4:18

Victor is an imprint of
Cook Communications Ministries, Colorado Springs, Colorado 80918
Cook Communications, Paris, Ontario
Kingsway Communications, Eastbourne, England

WHEN THE MAN YOU LOVE TREATS YOU
LIKE THE WOMAN HE HATES
© 2001 by David B. Hawkins

ISBN: 0-78143-475-0
First Printing, 2001
Printed in the United States of America

Editors: Greg Clouse, Craig Bubeck
Cover & Interior Design: Global Images and iDesignEtc.

# About the Author

A licensed clinical psychologist trained in the fields of social work and clinical psychology, Dr. David B. Hawkins, ACSW, Ph.D., has been in private practice for more than twenty years and specializes in domestic violence, adult and family issues, and marriage enrichment. Based in Longview, Washington, he is a certified domestic violence perpetrator treatment provider, certified forensic examiner, and a spiritual director. He also is a member of the National Association of Social Workers, Academy of Forensic Examiners, and the American Psychological Association. The author of several other books, including *See Dick and Jane Grow Up* (ISBN: 0-78143-498-X), David

cohosts a weekly radio program entitled "Experiencing Family," and was the host of an award-winning community television program called "Right Where You Live." He has been married to his wife, Diane (a nurse practitioner) for more than twenty-five years, and they have two grown sons. He enjoys snow and water skiing, hiking, kayaking, and running in recreational races in his free time.

*"Of what can be said when a man beats a woman
and she loves him anyway, or if she awaits him
while he sits in prison. . . .
Does this diminish the legitimacy of her love for him? . . .
Such events do not diminish the legitimacy of her love,
but rather increase its tragedy."*

—C.S. Lewis

# I͟NTRODUCTION

It has been said that love can heal anything. Certainly the greatest power in the world has to be love. What else matters if you do not have someone who loves you, and that you love in return? And isn't there within all of us at all times that ideal of wanting to be cared for, admired, and appreciated? Love, as they say, springs eternal in our hearts.

The issues addressed in this edition of **Your Pocket Therapist** have to do with the situation that unfortunately arises when there are more times of denigration than admiration; more times of carelessness than caring; more times of being ignored than appreciated. What does someone say to the woman who is told that she is cared for, but feels little of it? When her feelings and thoughts are continuously devalued, she feels abused and in extreme pain. These are the tough places in which many women live, and for which there are few easy answers. These times of devaluation may also remind her of times past when she felt put down, further intensifying the negative experience.

I am not addressing the black and white areas of physical and sexual abuse in this booklet. Such serious concerns require another level of discussion altogether, which we cannot tackle in this booklet without detracting from the important subject at hand. But when abuse becomes physical, a criminal act is usually involved, and society is more prepared to take a stand. Even so, society and the church can be slow to distinguish the lines of abuse, let alone take decisive action. Christians, of all people, should be prepared to confront sinful brutality.

This booklet is about the more subtle forms of abuse often perpetrated against women (though of course, not limited to women). It is not easy for a woman to say that she is being abused when there are no marks on her body, and she is being told that all of her frustration is in her mind. This enemy is hard to fight, and she more often than not finds herself fighting the person she knows best—herself!

Let me be clear about the use of the word *abuse*, because many cringe when they first hear that word. Can financial control and domination of the family resources equal abuse? Can being told that your memory is faulty be called abusive? Is having your feelings consistently discounted abusive? I believe that *abuse occurs when one adult unfairly attempts to control the environment, thoughts, and actions of another.* This is usually done through threats, intimidation, humiliation, or outright physical or verbal violence.

Unfortunately, some go as far as to use the Scriptures to maintain control over their spouses. Though there are passages that give a certain order to the family structure, abuse of power was never intended. It is very easy for the controlling person to use any weapon, including the Bible, to manipulate his spouse. The bottom line is that we are to love one another humbly and sacrificially, doing everything to meet the other's needs. Men are to love their spouses as Christ loved the church, and as their own bodies (Ephesians 5:25-28). Sadly, studies show that as much abuse exists within the church as outside.

Subtle forms of abuse abound. They are not limited to women, though this will be our focus here, as they are by far the most frequent victims. The reader may find that she too uses tactics that are designed to elicit control, all the while feeling innocent. Who is the victim and who is the villain? It becomes very confusing, and the roles may change at times, ranging from blame, to counterattack, to attack. Who is right and who is wrong? Who started it? If these issues sound familiar, you may be caught up in some very destructive patterns.

# THE SACRED SELF

I am approaching the topic of *self* with the belief that we are all made in the image of God and are therefore sacred and precious. No one deserves to be denigrated or profaned in any way. A relationship filled with shame, humiliation, blame, and subtle and overt put-downs is a direct violation of this biblical truth. Recognizing those put-downs and stopping them can be another matter, but understanding what is happening is an important first step.

Let's begin by examining these personal and sacred parts of ourselves. We will then look at how they are violated in an emotionally abusive atmosphere, noting how systematic, consistent belittling will undermine the very sacred core of a person.

# *Special*

"SO GOD CREATED MAN IN HIS
OWN IMAGE, IN THE IMAGE
OF GOD HE CREATED HIM;
MALE AND FEMALE
HE CREATED THEM."

—*Genesis 1:27*

**The Ability to Feel:** One sacred aspect of the self is the ability to have feelings. While you might not be aware of feelings and have not had practice in labeling them, they are constant nonetheless. Feelings are ubiquitous—they are present in every situation. Almost every thought that you have can elicit feelings. And of course, even memories elicit feelings.

On a more subtle level, there is a "feeling tone" in your home. Your environment has taken on a feeling that can be palpable at times. You must sit quietly and observe, however, to feel what is happening around you. Most often we scurry about so quickly that we fail to register our true reactions to events and circumstances.

Your ability to feel is a very deep and personal aspect of who you are. It is tied to your genetic makeup and history. It is tied to your personal life story. All the events that have occurred in your life will influence the inner self. To be aware of this sensitive part of yourself is touching on who you are as a person. To attend to and honor the feeling part of your self is a sacred thing.

When you stop to consider that feelings are the barometer that tells you what is happening in your life, they take on new importance. For example, feeling sad may be like a sharp pain or dull ache; it simply tells you that you are missing something or that there has been a significant loss in your life that needs attention. Likewise, if you do not take the time to attend to your sadness and loss, you may act in some other unconscious way to avoid this feeling. Your behaviors may, in some direct and possibly unknown way, be driven by your emotions. Like pain, your feelings are important to recognize. Your feelings are perhaps the most personal statement about you.

Jesus Himself had feelings, as He was like us in every way, being fully human. He was happy at the wedding at Cana, and celebrated with His friends. He was angry at those who desecrated the temple with shady business transactions. He was saddened at the death of His friend Lazarus. Finally, He was shaken with anguish in Gethsemane as He contemplated his death. He truly felt the entire range of human emotions and honored them.

**The Ability to Think:** You have been created incredibly—you're gifted with the capacity to think about events, and then process those thoughts. Your ability to think means you can see things for what they are. You can see the end results of certain actions.

You can predict the future to an extent. You can see the effect that actions have on the way that you feel. You have certain perceptions and judgments about things that again make you special and unique. You see the world differently from others.

I want to make a big deal about this thing called thinking. Many who have been put down repeatedly have been attacked for their supposed lacking ability to think. This defining attribute of personhood can be a prime target for someone who wants control. It actually makes strategic sense that a controlling person would attack your ability to think above anything else. Your perceptions and judgments may not make sense to him, and worse, may be threatening. But it's crossing the line of abuse when he feels the need to essentially brainwash you into believing you know nothing. He may demand that you choose his point of view as the right one. However, though he may think his is the wisest way, his intellectual bullying betrays him—wise people acknowledge their fallibility. Indeed, humility is the sign of strength; the clear sign of insecurity is when one demands the approval of another. However, empathy for one's opposition is a sign of maturity—true faith and conviction can endure disagreement.

For now I want to emphasize that you are unique and have unique perceptions. It is not necessary for anyone else to agree with that point of view or multiple points of view, but owning them is a right that you will need to give yourself. I want to encourage you to believe and affirm the following: *you know what you know;* it's as simple as that! You are a bright individual who can analyze events and see the effect they have on you and others. You can see what is happening and make sense out of it. In any case, you have the right to your own opinion.

**The Ability to Evaluate:** Perhaps here is where the human creature surpasses all other intelligence on the planet. You have the ability to not only feel your feelings and think things through, but also to evaluate these circumstances. You can, and do, make judgments about situations, determining if they are good or bad for you and others. You have a reality that is very personal. No one else will see things exactly the way that you do, and it is so important to embrace that unique reality. Your perceptions will not be the same as anyone else's, and if they are, you have probably worked long and hard to make sure that you do not stand out. Now may be the time to begin affirming your unique points of view.

"You need only claim the events
of your life to make yourself yours.
When you truly possess all
you have been and done,
you are fierce with reality."

—*Florida Scott-Maxwell*

Take just a moment now and think of a controversial topic. Any one will do: abortion, women's rights, war, women in the workplace, motherhood. Pick one! What do you think about any of these topics? Are you aware that your point of view will be unlike others'? Your particular slant on things will be unlike any one else. Can that be all right?

If you have a history of being denied your feelings, thoughts, and ability to know your own truth, this may be difficult for you. Now I am not saying that your point of view is always right. I *am* saying that you are perfectly all right for being just who you are. This may sound unbelievable, but it is true. Embrace your unique value. Be aware of your feelings, reflect, and then evaluate your position. This will require a safe place and a freedom and permission to do so. The permission will have to come from you. Can you give it to yourself?

It is important that you cultivate the ability to reflect. I often encourage my clients to keep a journal to assist them in the process of reflecting on their feelings, thoughts, and life circumstances. Given this time to reflect, I am confident that they will come to see what is important to them and avenues to enhance their lives. But you and I both know that taking the time to reflect, meditate on Scripture, and perhaps keep a journal, may be a luxury when you have an underlying feeling of fear and chaos in your home. If you have never done this, you may first have to overcome fear and inertia. It's worth it.

**The Ability to Decide:** In your natural, precious, unashamed state, you have the ability to feel, think, evaluate, and then make appropriate decisions. I am not saying that you will always make the best decisions, but you have the ability to make good decisions. This may be news to you, especially if you have been told repeatedly that you are "stupid" or "crazy," or that your choices are always poor ones. Not only do you have the ability to decide, you are probably the only person qualified to make a final decision in your behalf. You are familiar with your unique values, and God has made you the person that you are. No one else will ever know those subtleties about you.

Your ability to decide will in part be based on your ability to accept yourself the way you are. You have been "fearfully and wonderfully made"—no one else is quite like you. Being judgmental and self-critical will interfere with your ability to make healthy decisions. If you are overly self-conscious from excessive external or internal criticism, you will doubt yourself and be hesitant to make your own decisions. This will be an area of growth for your future. Before that can happen, however, you must be safe from any barrage of criticism that you may be experiencing. We will talk more about that later. For now it is enough that you affirm your ability to make decisions, which is a profound gift and responsibility. You can give that power away, but you can also reclaim it. You may want to take a moment right now to reclaim your ability to decide what is best for you. You may want to thank God for your ability to reason, evaluate, and make decisions.

**The Ability to Act:** After you have processed your feelings, thought about your situation, evaluated your problem, and prayerfully made a decision in your best interest, under optimal conditions you now have the ability to act. This is nothing short of incredible. You can make changes that will enhance your life.

You have the profound ability to see what works for you and what doesn't. Then you can make necessary adjustments for joyful living. Now understand that all of this is contingent on acceptance, both by yourself and those close to you. In short, you must feel safe. When people feel safe, they can take risks. If you are living in fear, you may feel restrained, closed, self-protective. This is natural, and we will talk more about this. For now, let it be sufficient to begin believing that you have the ability to act decisively in ways that will add meaning to your life.

You have been given the power to act. God has given you gifts and special skills to use for His purposes, and He desires that you be true to yourself (see Rom. 12:6). If you will act in a way that is consistent to your real self, others will be positively changed in the process. You have a unique contribution to make; in fact, some would say that you have an obligation to be true to yourself and make that contribution. It could get a little scary. That's why many choose to give up this power and live in the role of the victim, continuing to believe that they have no choices and must continue to live just the way that they do now. What will it be for you? Will you maintain the movement toward growth in your life? Stop for a moment and consider what are the ramifications of this outlook for your own life.

# THE IMPORTANCE
# OF SELF-AWARENESS

Self-acceptance begins with self-awareness. Who are you and what do you value? What do you feel and what is unique about you? How do you view the world differently than others you know? Have you been willing to share your true self with others? For that matter, have you had the opportunity to safely share things about yourself? Do you even think about yourself and what you need? Perhaps such thinking is new to you!

On the other hand, do you feel criticized and put down for who you are? Are you made to feel badly about your feelings, thoughts, or decisions? Do you live in fear, sometimes in ways that are difficult to describe? It is never too late to grow up and blossom into the person that you were designed to be. It is never too late to discover the special skills and talents that lie buried deep within. But growth for anything or anyone requires certain conditions. You will need to determine if those conditions have been present for you.

If you have been living in an atmosphere that does anything less than celebrate who you are—or worse, is thick with criticism—self-awareness may be a luxury. This should be no surprise since you are using all of your energy simply to cope, defend yourself, or create some semblance of safety. In the storm of your life, keeping the ship upright may be all you're capable of. Having the luxury of self-awareness is not possible. In this environment you are probably doing everything you can just to stay afloat . . . to keep the family running, maintain your job, keep the house in order. Self-realization may simply not be a possibility.

Right now can you set a goal to take some time each day to reflect on your life, your areas of freedom, and your areas of fear? Will you decide that you are valuable enough to create a future life that celebrates who you are? Spend time every day reflecting on Scripture, asking for wisdom, and seeking direction. If you will carve out even a little space in which you can feel unafraid, you will be able to think more clearly. Believe that as you seek wisdom God will empower you to understand His will for your life. Perhaps you can only set aside ten minutes a day at first. That's okay, because it is a start. Choosing to focus on your life will be a big step in and of itself. Personal and spiritual growth will follow!

# Growth

"IT IS NECESSARY TO TRY
TO SURPASS ONE'S SELF ALWAYS;
THIS OCCUPATION OUGHT
TO LAST AS LONG AS LIFE."

— *Queen Christina of Sweden*

# POST-TRAUMATIC STRESS DISORDER (PTSD)

If you have not thought about your needs, feelings, beliefs, and actions for a long time, when someone asks you how you are feeling, you may genuinely be stumped trying to answer. Your feelings have been frozen for so long that they cannot be thawed on command.

Another reason you may feel frozen in old patterns is called *Post-Traumatic Stress Disorder*. This fancy title means that an old destructive pattern has become an ingrained part of your life because something happened which was too difficult to fully experience at the time. You may have been traumatized so dramatically that you have frozen parts of yourself so that you could survive the pain. You may have been caught up in patterns of constantly defending yourself so that there is precious little energy left to create a life for yourself. Consequently, times and places will reawaken that pain and many of your actions may be unconsciously designed to avoid similar pain in the future.

In therapy sessions I often ask women if the patterns that they are currently experiencing fit any pattern that existed in any earlier marriage, or in their family of origin. Surprisingly few are able to talk about any patterns, because they have never really given that concept much thought. But it deserves thought now, because you may be living out a long-standing pattern of abuse and neglect.

It is important to review your life and honestly recall what you have experienced and the effect those experiences have had on you. Instead of continuing to distance parts of your life, you need to remember them and reconnect them to your current life experiences. These past experiences shape you and set a course upon which you may unconsciously remain, many times to your detriment. We all need, to the best of our ability, to be free from early trauma so that we can make healthy, conscious choices here in the present. If you are not making healthy choices, you may want to critically look at your earlier life to see if there is some old patterns that you are avoiding (PTSD) or some pattern that is familiar to you. If this experience feels too scary to you, do not hesitate to ask for help.

**Exercise:** Take a few minutes right now to look back and see if there are some patterns of abuse and neglect that need loving attention. You can do this in one of several ways. One of the easiest is to draw a family tree. Go back several generations and write down areas of concern on this tree. Of course, much of your focus will concern your biological parents and grandparents, as well as those of your spouse, if you can get that information.

List next to the person any incidences of emotional, sexual, or physical abuse or victimization. Note any alcohol or drug abuse. List any areas of emotional problems and make a special note whether or not these issues were addressed by the family. Was there openness about the issue or rather a tense secretiveness hiding something terrible under the surface? Did you know intuitively that issues existed that you did not dare approach?

Another part of the exercise can include what you learned from your family. What were the "rules" that governed your early behavior? For example, were the men the dominant ones in the family, while women were seen and not heard? Were the men abusers and the women tolerant stabilizers? Was there an unspoken expectation that you always be a good girl, ready to set your needs aside for others? Consider these patterns and others and decide what patterns may apply to your life. Write them down and name them. There is power in naming those things that have had a stranglehold on us.

Now take your new experience in claiming your reasoning abilities and *tell yourself the truth about these matters.* Yes, the old voices are strong and commanding, but you can now recognize your own voice, and it is the one that truly matters. Weigh out the old messages, and where they came from, as opposed to the new, inner honored voice of your own person. Get used to listening to yourself, and then listen to God—let go of the old, damaging voices from the past. *"Do not conform any longer to the pattern of this world, but be transformed by the renewing of your mind. Then you will be able to test and approve what God's will is—his good, pleasing, and perfect will"* (Rom. 12: 2).

Finally, take a few moments to consider what you have gained from those experiences. For those who love God, He promises nothing is wasted. Take a closer look to see what gold may be separated from the dross. For example, if you have been criticized incessantly, you may have also learned to be independent, knowing that your affirmations were not going to come from others. Perhaps you have developed a tenacity to weather most any storm. No Pollyanna here, since you have had to dig deep within to cope. Perhaps the challenges have sent you to your knees in prayer, resulting in an incredible spiritual booster. List a few of the blessings that you have reaped.

Let's now look at some of the ways that your freedom and value may have been or are now being diminished. It is important to note that these behaviors may not be intentional or with the conscious intent to hurt. The man in your life may be acting out patterns that he has lived by for years. It is likely a generational pattern that he too may find imprisoning at some level. He may also wish to be set free from the old patterns that tyrannize him. Whatever his feelings, it is time for the negative patterns to change. These patterns often have their origins in the past where the little boy was humiliated and taught that he was ineffective and powerless. Now bigger and older, he can at least act in control.

*Freedom*

"FREEDOM IS FRAGILE
AND MUST BE PROTECTED.
TO SACRIFICE IT,
EVEN AS A TEMPORARY MEASURE,
IS TO BETRAY IT."

—*Germaine Greer*

# Subtle Forms of Abuse

This booklet is about *subtle abuse*. Some of my clients have balked when I used the word abuse. The men have really disliked that word. Yet I have continued to use it for several reasons. For one, it gets attention. It has caused both the woman and man to think about the topic of abuse. Calling it anger or "temper problems" does not do justice to the underlying problems. They are larger than that and need real attention.

Secondly, I have continued to say it because I believe it is true. Those behaviors perpetrated upon another that are used purely to control and dehumanize are abusive. Behaviors that cause a loss of dignity are forms of abuse. I have also repeatedly found that these behaviors tend to escalate unless they are labeled as abusive, and decisive intervention is taken to stop it.

**Constant Criticism:** Many relationships are unfortunately filled with an atmosphere of criticism. The man, feeling out of control and inadequate in some way, must project these feelings onto others, and his wife may be the target. His perfectionism focuses on her, and she constantly feels as though she is not measuring up. Her self-worth may not be affected immediately, but erosion is taking place nonetheless.

At times this criticism may be quite subtle; at other times it may flare up quite dramatically as he makes it clear that certain attitudes or behaviors are not acceptable. His arguments have been so emotionally compelling, and the threat of his love being withdrawn seems so intimately connected to the situation, that over time his wife has to behave in the prescribed manner . . . at least most of the time. She learns well what is expected of her in order to be safe from his wrath and contempt. As she tiptoes through life, the loss of the sacred self is certain.

The criticism can take on a compulsive quality, ultimately continuing without interruption. Little thought seems to be given to the devastating impact of the critical attitude, partially because it is so compulsive: that is, done without thinking. An interruption of the pattern is needed—what I refer to as *decisive intervention.* Something that grabs his attention must be done to effect change. Half efforts avail nothing.

**Control**: One of the passive abuser's favorite weapons is control. He wants to be in control of everything, from how you think to how you act. In fact, one of the quickest ways of determining if this form of abuse is taking place is to take this test: How often do you say the words, "He allowed me to do that today"? Or conversely, "I'd better not do that, because he wouldn't like it." Of course the key issue here is being *allowed* to do something, as if you are not a free thinking and acting individual.

Now I do not want to be misunderstood on this topic. I am all in favor of treating one another with respect and talking to each other about your activities. It would not be appropriate to say to your spouse, "I'm going to do such and such whether you like it or not." That certainly shows disrespect, and none of us would want to be talked to that way.

I am also not promoting rebellion within the relationship. There is no value in having an I'll-do-my-thing-and-you-do-yours kind of relationship. There must be some order in the relationship, with mutual regard. The danger we are guarding against is when our spouse tells us, consistently, what we can and cannot do. In this atmosphere our individuality dies.

Of course, as you can see, a healthy tension can and should exist in the marriage. There is a fine balance to strive for that includes encouraging each of us to be ourselves, while at the same time being sensitive to our spouse's needs. This "tension" can make for an exciting, dynamic relationship.

**You Don't Know:** Another weapon that has incredible power is being told emphatically that you don't know what you know. That is what he would have you believe: things are not the way that they seem to you. He did not do what you know he has done. He does not criticize you as much as it seems to you. He did not yell at you the way you believe he yelled at you. He is not as harsh with the kids as you think. In short, what you believe is untrue. With the power of his words he rewrites history, and your version of it, to his thinking, is just wrong.

Worse yet, he blames you for exaggerating the truth. You are the one who is too lenient with the children; too tight or loose with money; too disagreeable and deserving of his criticism. You are the one to blame, not him. Therapists actually call this "*crazymaking*." The constant attack on your perceptions ultimately leads to self-doubt, and you may actually feel you are going crazy. The erosion of your self-esteem depletes your reserves and ability to fight back.

Even worse than his putting you down, you begin to put yourself down and believe that you truly are inadequate. His put-downs begin to find root and grow within you. Now not only is *he* against you, but *you* may have turned against yourself as well. You may continue to berate yourself and minimize your strengths, just as he has done for so long.

**Physical Violence, Threats, Intimidation**: Let me be clear. These are not subtle forms of abuse. These are the more blatant forms, though they may happen only periodically. Verbal intimidation, with the occasional push or physical threat, goes a long way in establishing control. Even mild physicality tells you that he could be explosive at any time, and you must always be on guard at some level. You must be on guard for public humiliation if you step out of line. You know you must tiptoe to be "safe."

Enough cannot be said about the power gained by one who has clearly established the pecking order through the use of abuse. He has made it clear that he is in charge and may erupt at any time. You have been made aware—by his threats, temper, sarcasm, pouting, withdrawal, and any number of other methods—that he is in charge.

Of course, I want to emphasize again that no form of violence should be tolerated. We know that violence, even occasional, escalates if no one puts a stop to it. In spite of the flowers and tears later, the abuse will happen again. *Intervention is the only sure means of ending the destructive patterns.* Sometimes it takes a physical separation to end this kind of abuse.

Intimacy, incidentally, is impossible when an abusive power

structure is in place. Intimacy is impossible when mutual respect is not established. You will never be totally free to blossom into your true self because you must always be wary of his moods and actions. You are never free from conflict so that you are simply free to grow. It is similar to a plant that never receives enough nourishment; it can exist without enough water for a while, but can never grow to its full potential.

**Don't Be Angry**: While it is clearly all right for others to be angry, you may have learned that your anger is not permissible. If you get angry, he gets angrier. He feels threatened with your anger and does not know how to deal with it. He may rage back at you, thus overwhelming you and making it unsafe to have healthy conflict with him. Anger and raging have proven to be useful techniques for him, in that they have won him another level of control.

Unfortunately, his anger may remind you of earlier experiences with anger in your life. Remember the idea of PTSD? You may have been conditioned to stuff your anger, or worse, to turn it against yourself. You may have learned early in life to blame yourself for any problems and avoid the conflict inherent in confronting others. But this only reinforces his power and the destructive patterns that exist. Now is the time to pay attention to your anger and use it as a changing force within you.

**Shifting the Blame**: Another tactic that you will undoubtedly recognize is the shifting of blame. Not only will many men not take responsibility for their actions, they feel compelled to blame others (you) for their problems. This can be in small and insignificant things as well as the larger issues.

This shifting of blame creates tremendous problems for a relationship. Obviously, if someone will not accept his portion of responsibility for a problem, it cannot then be resolved effectively. You may be experiencing a tendency to accept the blame for all things. Though you know intellectually that this is not reasonable, it can become a subtle and insidious pattern. You find yourself always wondering what you did wrong to create his bad mood. This pattern will erode your sense of well-being, not to mention reinforce his inappropriate pattern of blaming others.

**Controlling Your Friends and Activities**: Another method of inappropriate control, and thus abuse, is confining access to your friends and family. He fears they will cause you to question the environment he has created, and this threatens him. This also has the effect of isolating you, which increases his power and further diminishes your own. We all need feedback regarding our feelings and situation. If you are cut off from critical sources of support, your recovery will be hindered.

One of the ways he may control your friends and family is to criticize them incessantly. He may never actually forbid you to see them, but may always have something derogatory to say about them. You know that he doesn't want you to associate with certain people, and if you are threatened enough, you will strive to please him in this area too.

As you change one thing after another for him, what happens to the real you? Who do you become? Only as you recognize the damage that is happening to your personality will you be able to make changes to heal.

It is not unusual for me to see women who have successfully challenged a long-term destructive relationship and feel an incredible sense of relief and freedom, as well as excitement as they come to find their true self again. If you feel like you have lost a part of yourself in this relationship, it may have a great deal to do with these subtle but long-standing patterns of abuse.

**Your Needs Are Ignored**: As you consider your relationship to an abusive man, you will come to see the pattern of his self-centeredness. You may feel at times that you must always focus on his life and his needs, and when you do not, you pay a price. You may find a deep level of resentment developing within as you recognize that no one is asking about *your* needs. You may find that you have primary responsibility for caring for the home, the family, and him, with little left over to care for yourself. You may find that he does not really concern himself with your well-being, and if you do have a need, you are encouraged to get over it soon.

Sometimes this pattern becomes so prominent that if you display any weakness, such as crying, it will bring outright criticism from him. Your vulnerability is, again, too threatening to him. He does not seem to have the resources to care for himself and you too. He has grown accustomed to having your world revolve around him.

Does this pattern fit you? Are you able to openly accept your own feelings without losing them in his needs? It is at once very subtle and damaging to relinquish your emotions and needs to him and the family. It may take special care to again look within and rebuild your sense of self. More importantly, you can be sure that as you begin to take back some of your lost ground, he will become very threatened.

**Jealousy:** A closely related topic to the previous one is that of jealousy—rampant, outrageous, out-of-control jealousy. Perhaps he has been hurt in a previous marriage or relationship and now projects many of those issues on you. Until he faces those past hurts and losses, you will be paying the price. Furthermore, encouraging him to look at those issues will probably fall on deaf ears until he is motivated to improve the relationship.

Jealousy becomes very suffocating. He may be threatened by friends, activities, even the way you look. He may try to control how you dress or the way you wear your hair. If it is not the way he likes it, he may become suspicious and question your motives. In short, it can become a never-ending circle of accusations, attacks, blame-placing, and threats until you conform. You must remember that jealousy does not mean love. Love means trust; suspicious and demeaning behavior does not speak of trust. You also need to be aware that these patterns are not necessarily continued out of meanness, but rather to preserve his shaky sense of well-being and urgent need for control.

**The Little Boy:** All the while that he is using abusive tactics, something inside tells you that he is not very happy with himself. You can see that and sense that in some ways you are stronger than he is and must do something to bolster his flagging ego. All of the macho stuff feels and looks like raw power, and it is intimidating. Yet you know that underneath the bravado is a boy who really needs you. He needs you to find him adorable, smart, and most importantly, *right*. Unfortunately, this may become something that you begin to enjoy, perpetuating the destructive relationship patterns. Perhaps you have needed someone to care for, re-creating an old pattern for you.

Guilt seems to be an integral part of the pattern. Sensing his inability to live without you, you may repeatedly "forgive" his outbursts and controlling behaviors. You may be feeling guilty for even thinking about leaving the relationship or seriously confronting him about his behavior. This guilt, however, is misguided and enables the situation to remain the same.

Another part of the pattern is often the fact that he can be so charming and sorry for his behavior at times. If he were a brute, you say to yourself, you would leave him in a minute. But he is not. He can be loving, and this can create much confusion within you. What is the matter with you that you feel so many confusing and negative feelings that do not go away? There is something within him that tugs at your maternal heartstrings, for you know better than others how truly needy he is on the inside. After all the pain he can be so loving and attentive, and the destructiveness almost feels worth it all.

**Caretaker:** Because he can be so charming, and yet so needy at the same time, you have probably developed the skill of caretaking down to a fine science. Preposterous as it seems, many times you may find yourself wondering, "Where would he be without me?" Indeed, your perceptions are quite accurate, because often a codependent relationship has developed where both spouses are meeting some need of the other. Certainly, beneath his bravado he needs you. Your intuition correctly tells you that. But somewhere in the hidden parts of yourself, you may have grown accustomed to needing and taking care of him as well.

The role of caretaker is one that greatly diminishes both parties. It is a way of saying, "I know that you cannot live without me, and so I will always be there to take care of you." What a subtle put-down this is.

Now I know that to some of you what I have just said may be jarring. What do I mean that caretaking is a problem? Are we not called to take care of one another? Well, yes and no. I do not believe that we are called to "mother" our spouse. By "mothering" him we create a very unhealthy way of relating to one another. Rather we are called to "care" for one another; being sensitive to his needs, but allowing him to work out some of his own issues.

**Why You Stay:** This issue has been used to beat up women for a long time. Abused women criticize themselves unmercifully for staying, when it seems like it should be simple to leave. So since many cannot leave, they must be weak in character, right? Wrong!

Leaving can be a very difficult thing to do, especially after years of abuse and codependency. Many threads often keep this tattered cloth together. Someone has likened it to a beaten dog that is loyal to its master no matter what the treatment. One gradually grows accustomed to the bad treatment, and healthy care for oneself must be learned again.

So do not berate yourself for having stayed in a destructive relationship. Furthermore, do not listen to those who offer simple platitudes on how you can make your life better. If they have been there, you will sense their understanding. If they haven't, kindly tell them to take their advice elsewhere.

Furthermore, you may sense that God wants you to remain committed in spite of the turmoil. This is a time when sensitivity to what God wants you to do is so very critical. Often it is possible to stay in the relationship and yet begin to act differently, changing the entire "system."

# TAKING INVENTORY

We have made quite a list of possible areas of subtle abuse. Take a few moments now and consider which of these patterns may fit your life and marriage relationship. You cannot change anything unless you have looked in the mirror and courageously decided what really needs to change. Below are a few of the patterns that we have discussed which may fit your situation.

- He blames me for everything that goes wrong.
- He puts down or controls access to my friends and/or family.
- He controls the way our money is spent.
- I feel responsible for his bad moods and feelings.
- I accept the blame for problems that are not mine.
- I alter my behavior to please him.

- He has been physically and/or verbally abusive with me;

- My needs are ignored;

- My opinions are ignored or put down.

(See the end of this booklet for a more complete inventory of abusive behaviors.)

As you review the list, you will get a sense if you are in an overtly or subtly abusive relationship. If you are, life is not over. You can change, and there are specific tools that you can use to create a healthy life for yourself. The suffering that you may have been through can be grist for the change mill. Let's look at how you can take new responsibility for your life.

# Making the Necessary Changes

Have you made the decision that you have been in an abusive relationship, in one form or another? That is the first step toward change. Take a moment now to renew again your decision to move forward in your life. The only person that you can change is you. Accept the fact that you cannot change him—in no way, shape, or form. You must be really clear about that. But you certainly can make changes of your own that will have an impact on him. He will not make changes without your taking decisive action. This is the first step.

**You Can Change:** You have probably felt more than your share of discouragement over the years. Perhaps many times you have vowed to end the abuse, only to find yourself right back in the middle of it. You have been told that you cannot change anything. Do not believe it. The very fact that you are reading this booklet is a testimony to your desire to change. Remember that you have many resources at your disposal to help you change. Others have been in your situation and are ready to help. (Look for the Women's Resource Center in your city.)

Sometimes we must reach bottom before we will look for outside help. Perhaps you are at the bottom now and are ready to take the following suggestions. One step at time, and soon you will notice change happening. God does not want anything less than for you to become all you were intended to be.

**Take Note of Your Relationship to Him:** One of the first things to do is nothing. Simply review the previous list (and the one at the end of this booklet) and see which attributes fit him and you. Watch how he treats you. In what ways is he abusive? What is your reaction to his abuse? How do you feel and how do you respond to your feelings? Do you accept your feelings, or do you minimize them? Take some time to simply observe and listen to your heart. Hold the entire situation before the Lord in prayer and ask for guidance.

**Journal:** Yes, I know that you have probably not kept a diary since high school. And you may have reasonable fears that someone will find your writings. It is true that your journal needs to be something safe and sacred for you, or else you cannot use it to say what really needs to be said. Nonetheless, this can be a place for you to say, perhaps for the first time, what is really happening to you.

> "YOU NEVER FIND YOURSELF
> UNTIL YOU FACE
> THE TRUTH."
>
> —*Pearl Bailey*

*Truth*

A journal can be an important place to begin to speak the truth for yourself. Especially if you have been living life on someone else's terms, losing yourself in the process. Grab a notebook or a book especially designed for journaling and begin to write your story. This is for you, for your clarity, and for honoring your truth. Just do it!

**Write Out the List of Abuses:** It is important to tell it like it is, though this assignment can be very painful. Write down and own the damage that is being done. Taking a close look at the abuse takes tremendous courage. You may be very tempted, like he is, to minimize what has happened to you. How exactly have you been victimized? How have you participated in the crazy-making? How have you been too frightened to make any changes? How have you enabled him to stay the way he is?

Write it out. Then review your journal entries to see where you have wanted to lessen the severity of the situation. Add the complete truth to it.

**Seek Support:** Now that you have started to clarify what is happening and the history behind it, you need to acknowledge it and find support for the difficult changes that lie ahead. You cannot go it alone. Go ahead and say it: "I cannot go it alone!" You will need guidance, support, and affirmations for the journey. Remember, as you seek to change, he will match your energy with pressure to abandon your efforts. It will *not* be easy.

Support can be found in a group therapy situation, in a support group, or perhaps with a good friend who can relate to your issues. Your pastor can be a valuable resource as you seek answers to difficult questions. But do find someone who has been where you are, or who you can trust completely to assist you in your journey. You are not alone.

**Decide that You Deserve to Be Treated with Dignity:** This is a mind-set that you will begin to carry with you wherever you go. It becomes an inner attitude, a growing strength that increases your esteem. You are sacred and deserve to be treated with respect, not only in your primary relationship, but in every relationship. Expect to be treated with respect and confront anyone who treats you otherwise.

Decide also that your thoughts, feelings, and decisions are invested with dignity. They are a composite of who you are and should not be just like everyone else's. Decide that you will celebrate these unique parts of who you are.

# Dignity

"I'LL KEEP MY PERSONAL DIGNITY AND
PRIDE TO THE VERY END—IT'S ALL I HAVE
LEFT, AND IT'S A POSSESSION THAT ONLY
I MYSELF CAN PART WITH."

*—Daisy Bates*

# UMMARY

I can imagine that this booklet has been emotionally charged for some of you. It may have reminded you of a troubling place in which you have been living far too long. But the hope of it all is that you have, at some level, been preparing for change. Not yet ready in times past, you are now ready to take another step forward. That is how we change—in a step-by-step development. While we would like to change once and for all, this is not the way it works. It all happens in process, and that is where you may be. So rejoice in the process!

Please do not be discouraged about your future. Taking the actions recommended in this booklet does not mean the end of your relationship with your spouse. It means the end of your relationship as you have known it. Yes, changes are waiting for you as you clear out the old and prepare for the new. Now your relationship will have the possibility of being healthy, life-giving, and sacred. As you change, he may very well change too! As you pray for your relationship, you will find that God may do a miracle in both of your lives.

Finally, this topic has to do with boundaries. It has to do with getting clearheaded about who you are and who you are not; with what you can change and what you cannot change; with what is your business and what isn't. As a way of finishing this booklet I will cite one of my favorite poems that gives me strength and clarity. You have heard of it, I am sure, and I hope that you find the meaning in it that I have found. Blessings on your journey!

# THE SERENITY PRAYER

God, grant me the serenity to accept the things I cannot change,

the courage to change the things I can,

and the wisdom to know the difference.

Living one day at a time, enjoying one moment at a time;

accepting hardship as a pathway to peace;

taking, as Jesus did, this sinful world as it is,

not as I would have it;

trusting that You will make all things right

if I surrender to Your will;

so that I may be reasonably happy in this life

and supremely happy with You forever in the next.

—*Reinhold Niebur*

# SHARE YOUR STORY

Throughout the development of this book series, we have been introduced to many exceptional individuals. We are interested in hearing your stories. We want to share your experiences so that we in turn can share them with others. Please send your thoughts to:

**Your Pocket Therapist**
Dr. David B. Hawkins
1801 First Avenue, Suite 3B
Longview, WA 98632
(360) 425-3854

Dr. Hawkins has established an exciting web site that offers encouragement for families. The site features help on family issues, links to other relevant sites, and information about setting up seminars or speaking engagements.

Visit his ministry at www.InCourageMinistry.com.

# Recommended Reading

Beattie, Melody. *Codependent No More.* Hazelden Foundation, 1987.

Forward, Susan and Torres, Joan. *Men Who Hate Women and the Women Who Love Them.* New York: Bantam Books, 1986.

Jeffers, Susan. *Feel the Fear and Do It Anyway.* New York: Fawcett Columbine, 1987.

Hemfelt, Robert, et al. *Love Is a Choice.* Nashville: Thomas Nelson Publishers, 1989.

Norwood, Robin. *Women Who Love Too Much.* New York: Simon and Schuster, Inc., 1985.

Oliver, Regina Madonna and Meehan, Bridget Mary. *Affirmations From the Heart of God.* Liquori Publications, 1998.

# APPENDIX
## INVENTORY OF ABUSE

Please note to what degree the behaviors fit for your situation.

1. I have been called derogatory names.

2. I have been excessively criticized, feeling like I cannot do anything right.

3. My friends have been criticized.

4. I have been discouraged from seeing, and denied access to my friends.

5. My relatives have been called names or criticized.

6. I have been told that I do not know anything.

7. I have been told that I could never make it on my own.

8. I have been kicked, hit, or slapped.

9. My spouse has thrown objects, especially those of importance to me.

10. My spouse has broken things, like doors or walls.

11. My spouse has threatened that if I left I would lose everything.

12. Our children have been used against me.

13. Our children have witnessed, or heard, the abuse in our home.

14. My spouse has slapped, hit, pushed, or kicked our children.

15. My spouse has called our children derogatory names.

16. I have been controlled with our money.

17. My spouse always wants to know what I am doing and checks up on me.

18. I have been discouraged from getting a job outside the home.

19. I am afraid of my spouse.

20. I am told that I have no reason to be afraid.

21. My outside activities/friendships have diminished.

22. My spouse does not seem to value my opinion.

23. My spouse makes decisions without my input.

24. I have a history of being abused.

25. My spouse has threatened to harm me.

26. My spouse has manipulated me sexually.

27. My spouse has threatened me with guns/weapons.

28. I am afraid to tell anyone what is really happening in our home.

29. I have lost self-confidence.

30. I have lost respect for my spouse.

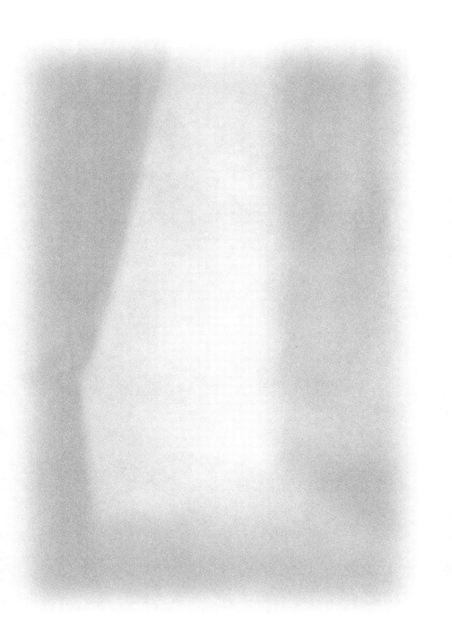